Poetic Day In the Life of A. Cat

Jodi Oden

McJamnes Press

Cat Loves You

I think of you in the morning

I think of you at night

You are the center

Of my world

My hero shining bright

Cat on Sleeping

I sleep which means

Move thou not

Yet once more

You disturb

Eliciting my voice

Translate:

Perturbed

Perturbed

Perturbed!

Cat Stretching

Turn around

Turn around

Stop and clap

Touch your toes

And ease

Ease

Ease

On back

Cat Has Waited a Whole Five Minutes for the Meal to be Served

Turn Around

Turn Around

Stop and Stomp

Paws on hips

And

Whomp

Whomp

Whomp

Cat Plays

Dance in the day

Dance in the day

Dancing will make

Your fur float away

Dance in the night

Dance in the night

Spread your pedals

And JUMPING, take flight

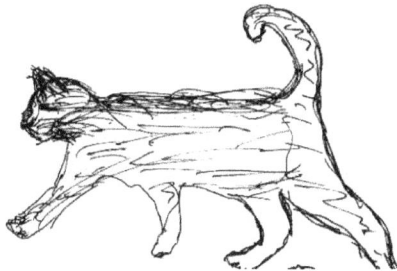

Cat Sniffs a Rose

A sniff from a rose

A rose, a rose

Waffles the nose

Wiggles the toes

Warms the day

From beginning to close

Cat in the Sun

O' glorious patches

Of sunshine

Glistening grass or floor below

I would sit and bathe

And bask away

Golden rays you do bestow

Cat Rolling

Rolling around

On the ground

My tummy plainly seen

Comfortable is

O gee whiz

I now have to be preened

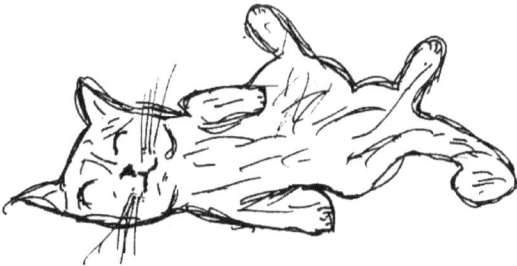

Cat Saw a Snake

I saw a snake

One that makes

That awful hissing sound

Sorry snake

My mistake

But I hope that you

May

Drown

Cat Liking Sight of Reflection in a Puddle of Water

Eyeing you

Is what I do

Aren't I cute

'Cause you're a hoot

Cat vs. Fly

A fly must die
That's all there is
To really understand it

So with my paw
His life snuff out
Leave you to write an obit

Cat vs. Mouse

Who created the mouse

Preying upon this house

Entertainment but so dumb

I abhor this thing

It squeakily sings

Amply eating his weight in crumbs

Cat is Patiently Waiting for You to Come Home

Two bits

Four bits

Six bits

Seven

Eight bits

Nine bits

Ten

And Eleven!

(Repeat, repeat, repeat!)

Cat When Human Finally Comes Home and It's Snack Time

These snacks

You act an interesting way

When with your arm

You're tossing

They are mine you know

So you may go

Your mind I'm sure

You're lossing

Cat On Catnip

My mind is moving

A swiftly mile a minute

Felt Really Bad

When I found

'Twernt nothing in it

Cat Song

Mew, mew

Meow, meow

Meow, meow, meow

Me, me

Me, me, me

Ew, ew, me, me

OW

Cat's Human Entering the Same Room

With Cat

My human comes in

Wearing a grin

I shan't pretend to know

So I just pass

This human mass

Ignoring his one man show

Cat on a Windowsill

On the sill

I chill

A spot where I lay quite a lot

Often I play

With all passersby

Whether they see me or not

Cat is Thinking of You

No Strings Attached

I love you

I said it

You pet me some more

And love me all the same

My heart holds true

Your face and smile

Burn on eternal flame

Cat Wants Food

Food Food

Food Food

My needs are not confusing

I ponder plate

Is "almost" bare

And what you find amusing

Cat Has Been Patient AGAIN for at Least a Minute Waiting

'Tis food I want

'Tis food I'll have

If you want peace and quiet

Must think me mad

You act a tad

Like I must starve and diet!

Cat Pose

I try to be regal

You said I was pretty

Or handsome as case may be

I pose and I pose 'cause I always knows

You love this admiring thing

So Queen may I be or if I'm a he

A King, A King, A King

No matter which way

I am here today

Requiring your kiss and bowing

Cat Phenomena

Hairballs

Hairballs

Yuck, yuck, yuck

Cough it

Cough it

Up, up, up

Nothing more to

Say or add

'Cept they bother

Bad, bad, bad

Cat Needs a Cuddle

Mine eyes have twinkled

At the thought

Of You

Holding Me

So close

And even closer still

Ah me, loving thee

Cat Gazes at the Moon

Space is a place

And cowboys race

Both take something

Called an Orbit

One is a horse

And one is a ship

They just pick a spot

And move toward it

Cat Says Goodnight

Darkness is upon us

Time to say goodnight

Wake up in the morning

See food from

New light

Cat Dreams

Dreaming while sleeping

Of playing with vice

Not allowed

To touch

As far as you know

'Tis only a dream

Acting on it

Not much

Cat Plays at Night

Playing at night

Is my delight

While you're sound asleep

It's only my way

Ending my day

Restoring my soul, my upkeep

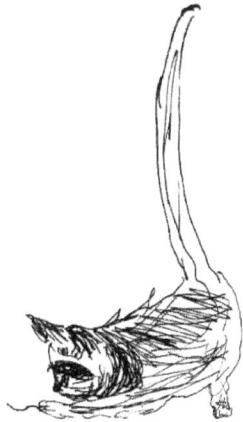

Cat Had Fun Playing and It Didn't Go With the Décor Anyway

Yes ma'am

No sir

And it wasn't me

When somethin' lay

Broken

As smashed up as can be

Cat's Life Basically

Outside, Inside

Inside, Out

What my life is all about

'Cept sleeping, eating

Pee, pee, peeing

Petting, playing

All this relating

Cat's life Cat's life

Is for me

I'm a fine cat

You agree?

Stay cool, cats....

Carry on,

--Arthur Cat

www.ingramcontent.com/pod-product-compliance
Lightning Source LLC
Chambersburg PA
CBHW071733020426
42331CB00008B/2013